Wilson Reading System®
Student Reader
Eleven

THIRD EDITION

by Barbara A. Wilson

Wilson Language Training Corporation
www.wilsonlanguage.com

Wilson Reading System® Student Reader Eleven

Item # SR11AB

ISBN 1-56778-077-6

THIRD EDITION (revised 2004)

The Wilson Reading System is published by:

Wilson Language Training Corporation
175 West Main Street
Millbury, MA 01527
United States of America

(800) 899-8454

www.wilsonlanguage.com

Printed in the U.S.A.

Step 11 Concepts

Additional I, E, Y Vowel Work

11.1 **y** in open, closed, v-e syllables (**reply**, **gym**, **type**)

11.2 The **Y** spelling rule (**enjoyable**, **player**)

11.3 **i** in an open syllable /ē/ (**orient**), **i** pronounced as /**y**/ (**million**, **genius**)

11.4 **ie/ei** (**piece**, **ceiling**, **vein**)

11.5 **igh**, **eigh** (**light**, **eight**)

y-closed

gym	symbol	gypsy
system	crystal	gymnastics
cymbal	gypsums	sympathy
Lynn	symptom	lynx
syllable	Flynn	sympathetic

y-vowel

hyphen	Styrofoam	community
sympathy	reply	fancy
cycle	agency	cyclone
lady	gypsy	dynamite
gymnastics	supply	city

A

y = /ī/

supply	magnify	occupy
horrify	deny	reply
occupy	clarify	rely
signify	identify	apply
multiply	classify	unify

B

y = /ī/

solidify	verify	amplify
gratify	rarefy	sanctify
pacify	crucify	fortify
comply	stupefy	justify
imply	electrify	defy

gyp	cyst	myth
syllabus	symbolic	pygmy
hymnist	lymph	mystic
syndrome	synopsis	physics
synthetic	syntax	cystic

y-closed

systematic	lynch	gypsum
symphony	analytic	pyx
crypt	sync	hysteric
syndicate	hypnosis	Sylvan
cynic	physics	sycamore

byte	enzyme	type
style	pyre	lyre
prototype	hype	analyze
electrolyte	megabyte	neophyte
electrolyze	hydrophyte	typeset

y-vowel

hydrogen	gypsum	Kyle
electrolyte	synopsis	astrology
cyanide	geology	mystic
lynch	hydrant	occupy
contingency	deny	ancestor

synt	metony	gyllope
prodyme	styme	cymote
stymest	crothy	plotryne
crytley	blyst	slemy
muntly	tymirt	shymp

phyllon	shymote	croby
spyle	syntem	cyment
trymote	spyle	pryst
closhy	chontly	flymelt
flyst	systop	stype

1   When Ben finished at the gym, he was starving.

2   I think you have the symptoms of the bad flu.

3   Mrs. Flynn stressed the importance of the task.

4   Mom was quite sympathetic when I told her my problem.

5   Ken could not miss his gymnastics class.

6   Tom would like to study geology, but Lynn plans to study physics.

7   The little baby seems to have the flu symptoms.

8   To read a difficult word, it is helpful to divide it into syllables.

9   Kyle hopes to take a gymnastic class this spring.

10   We won the crystal ball at the fair.

1   Mrs. Halpin was the gypsy who witnessed the big event.

2   Yolanda plans to develop a more systematic method for billing clients.

3   At times, Wendy wished that her husband was not so analytic.

4   Jane developed a cyst on her back and had to go to the clinic in the city.

5   Tom is such a cynic, he will probably think we're doing this for profit.

6   The author has a syndicated column which appears in the daily newspaper.

7   My boss desires to see a synthetic phonics approach in all the classes.

8   The class requested a more realistic syllabus.

9   I have always enjoyed going to the symphony with my dad.

10 The walls in my room are constructed with gypsum board.

1   Steve had lots of difficulty studying enzymes in his biology class.

2   Jane expressed herself with her style of dress.

3   Kyle went to the agency and had them type his syllabus.

4   The city of Memphis must carefully analyze its spending.

5   Mr. Hyde distracted the hymnist while she sang her solo.

6   Mom had to hype the family to trace its ancestry.

7   We'll type the report and make our decision over the weekend.

8   Typesetting is quite an involved task.

9   Our company recently procured a two hundred megabyte hard disk for the computer.

10 We must examine the prototype before we can purchase the item.

1   Rosa will apply for the open position at that company.

2   Can you classify the document in this file?

3   If you multiply those numbers, you will get the solution.

4   The supply of food is running out.

5   It is important to quickly reply to that message.

6   I must not rely on that source of information.

7   The troops haven't developed a plan to occupy that territory.

8   You can't deny that this project is a challenge.

9   The detective must find a witness to identify the killer.

10 We committed to the rules and now we must comply.

Exercise for Health

Donna Flynn went to the gym at least three times a week. She realized how important exercise was to her health. Ms. Flynn had a system that she followed. First, she would stretch out. Next, she pedaled several miles on a bicycle at the gym. Donna then swam ten free-style laps in the Olympic-size pool. She felt extremely refreshed when she finished! This young woman had the type of commitment needed to maintain her shape.

Many Americans have been into a "health kick" over the past decade. They have been more aware of the need to stay fit. People analyze their food intake more carefully and try to exercise. Donna sets a good example. It's vital to one's health to develop a positive exercise program in today's comfortable world!

y (no change)

tomboys	valleys	jerseys
swayed	enjoyable	payment
delayed	boyish	joyful
trayful	trolleys	kidneys
stayed	destroying	playful

y (change to *i*)

dried	happily	nastier
sloppiness	luckiest	copier
messiest	dirtiest	silliest
hobbies	carried	married
fried	frostiest	happier

pennies	pansies	babies
families	berries	candies
ladies	copies	factories
sixties	studies	cities
puppies	hurries	tries

y + ing

studying	carrying	babying
worrying	trying	copying
hurrying	frying	marrying
crying	drying	babyish
scurrying	emptying	magnifying

y (no change)

employment	praying	graying
dismayed	volleying	portraying
monkeying	joyous	wayward
decaying	employing	annoyed
convoys	straying	deployed

y (change to *i*)

glorious	soggiest	magnified
tallied	applied	plentiful
sloppily	harmonious	replied
implied	niftiest	tanginess
dressier	pestiness	carrier

liberties	territories	agencies
navies	flies	flurries
spies	marries	forties
parties	rallies	cries
studies	tallies	entries

y + ing

fiftyish	applying	rallying
relying	defying	caddying
identifying	prying	gratifying
replying	tarrying	supplying
ferrying	tallying	implying

Mixed

ladies	stormiest	enemies
loveliest	copied	enjoyable
drier	staying	keys
flying	laziest	cries
turkeys	player	ponies

delaying	replying	graying
counties	repayable	glorious
greediness	victorious	reliable
annoyed	industrious	galleys
luxurious	merriment	duties

plineys	bersier	conboyable
stoying	droftiest	blavies
regnified	prolayable	carniness
sterried	stomeyed	flerries
ploggiest	blessied	stolleying
plocayed	streyed	robeyment
plastier	stoyful	shallying
stomying	streniment	libneying
survoyed	flubies	stobbies
gloftier	proflayed	clobier

1   Dad lost his keys to the apartment.

2   The sunshine is so enjoyable.

3   The planes are delayed due to the snowstorm.

4   We need to make a payment on these books.

5   The monkeys are the best animals in the zoo.

6   We've stayed up later than our bedtime.

7   James keeps destroying my castle made of blocks.

8   Our football jerseys are drying in the sun.

9   The birthday party was a joyous occasion.

10   Barney Bear is such a playful puppy!

1   Jenny decided to make the silliest costume possible.

2   James fried the shrimp after dipping it in batter.

3   Roy married a girl that he met in Germany.

4   Jim has the messiest desk I have ever seen!

5   The picnic was held on a glorious day in late spring.

6   Jane bundled her children in winter coats on the frostiest morning this year.

7   I saved my pennies for this rainy day trip.

8   Americans should be thankful for their many liberties.

9   The garden is bright with red, yellow and pink pansies.

10   Flurries are expected in the Northeast this evening.

y + ing

1   You've helped me by emptying the trash.

2   I think your complaint seems babyish.

3   Doreen is studying for her spelling test.

4   Tony isn't worrying about the upcoming storm.

5   The baby is still crying.

6   Hasn't Larry been drying dishes in the kitchen?

7   Copying the list takes a long time.

8   I think we should be hurrying to get to the concert.

9   The scurrying chipmunk collected nuts to last throughout the winter.

10 A grayish-white squirrel stored his food in the tree for the winter.

1 The boys played in the park all afternoon.

2 Jane seems happier now than I can ever remember.

3 We emptied the desks in order to clean them.

4 Those beagle puppies are the cutest I've ever seen.

5 The swing swayed in the wind.

6 Rasheem feels like the luckiest man.

7 The kids are collecting berries in a basket.

8 The cities on the east coast are covered with snow.

9 That girl is marrying a rock star.

10 I've noticed that you're the laziest kid on Fridays.

y (no change)

1   Hopefully, unemployment will continue to decline in the nation.

2   The children are monkeying around in the den.

3   That autobiography portrayed him as a fine citizen.

4   The tennis players are volleying for the serve.

5   Our telephone payment is due this Tuesday.

6   Paul's boyhood was quite enjoyable while he lived along the seashore.

7   The hurricane winds destroyed much property along the eastern coast.

8   Audrey's train to Vancouver will be delayed for three hours.

9   Dad was annoyed when he could not find his hammer.

10 Many people are praying for peace in the world.

y (change to *i*)

1   The company will be renting a copier soon.

2   I will happily contribute to the preparation of the feast.

3   Barb is the happiest lady since she married her husband, Ed.

4   The U.S. carrier will be stationed in the harbor over the weekend.

5   The ladies and gentlemen will gather in the hall for the grand presentation.

6   Hopefully, more people in the cities and towns across the nation will soon be reading.

7   The cries of the homeless people must be heard.

8   The factories in this city are shutting down, and many people are unemployed.

9   Cara tries hard to do well in her studies.

10 Ted passed away in his late sixties due to lung cancer.

1 Paula has been trying to get that job for the past ten weeks.

2 Replying to the letter, Steve angrily mailed his response.

3 Mr. Green will be identifying the important information for the quiz.

4 Peg had to take a break from studying so she went to the campus party.

5 I think Phil will make quite a bit of cash by caddying at the local golf club.

6 There is no need for worrying about the algebra quiz – it will not be difficult.

7 Ed is tallying the score, but I have a feeling I am victorious.

8 Mom is hurrying supper by frying the fish.

9 The outrageous rallying continued throughout the night.

10 The stout man helped by emptying the heavy trash cans.

1 I had an enjoyable time when Jim and Peg were married.

2 Our company plans to install a new copying system.

3 The boss felt quite dismayed when he was given the latest sales report.

4 The food is plentiful so I truly hope you can join us.

5 I think Jake and Steve have the dirtiest jerseys on the team!

6 Mom plans to stop carrying her credit card.

7 Dad has applied for the sales job that will cover a wide territory.

8 We were flying to Alabama, but now our trip has been delayed.

9 That team always rallies in the last inning when playing at home.

10 The factories keep shutting down and laying off employees.

State Fair!

Empty grounds are raised into a bustle of activity. Families begin to arrive from counties across the state. The year-long planning and labor is now visible and demonstrated clearly. A state fair begins!

So much happens in a few days' time. One goal of these events is to promote the industries of the state. This is accomplished in the midst of much enjoyment. There are competitions including horse shows and tractor pulls. Ladies and gents present their kitchen masterpieces. The entries are judged, and blue ribbons are proudly worn. There are exhibitions and many displays. Amusement rides and games attract people of all ages. Music can be heard throughout the fairgrounds.

A state fair, in any state, is truly a joyful event!

Desert Sensation

Most people think the desert holds little color. People picture miles of sand with occasional rocky ledges and cactus plants. However, these hot, arid places are capable of exploding with various hues. This is infrequent, but quite glorious when it happens!

The conditions for flowering desert plants are not always ideal. They require an adequate amount of winter drizzle combined with a proper balance between hot and cold springtime temperatures.

The otherwise bland desert can be transformed into a sensational sight of harmonious color. Brittlebush may suddenly bloom into a golden carpet. One of the loveliest combinations is an orange poppy surrounded by purple-hued lupine. A cliff can become a colorful sight with a flowering, twisted shrub called a cliff rose.

When the desert displays itself in such glory, it provides a most gratifying glimpse of the marvels contained in all forms of life.

familiar	million	savior
follows	onion	union
behavior	Pennsylvania	senior
ammonia	junior	brilliant
Virginia	genius	billion

Daniel	begonia	rebellion
spaniel	California	opinion
convenient	trillion	reunion
stallion	peculiar	gardenia
companion	civilian	lenient

A

i = /ē/

piano	obedient	geranium
Indian	scorpion	stadium
champion	Philadelphia	medium
studio	obedience	comedian
radiator	Maria	radio

B

i = /y/

minion	alienation	medallion
battalion	communion	genial
billiards	valiant	brilliantly
galliard	vermilion	pavilion
pinion	disunion	zillion

radius	ruffian	tibia
podium	aviation	alleviate
medial	opium	amiable
inebriate	trivial	finial
trivia	phobia	tapioca

radial	palladium	aviator
mediate	phobia	zodiac
cardiogram	Orient	trio
obvious	radiate	cranium
appropriate	recipient	menial

uranium	patriotic	cranial
condominium	radiator	median
remedial	cardiac	radiant
Oriental	enunciate	repudiate
audio	claustrophobia	cilia

i = /ē/

fiesta	amphibious	affiliate
deviate	mediator	calcium
effluvium	alien	radiance
jovial	equilibrium	capriole
Kodiak bear	ganglia	ambiance

minicam	semidesert	anticommunist
minibike	antiaircraft	semifixed
minicomputer	antipoverty	semiformal
minicar	antidemocratic	semi-independent
minibus	antislavery	semiconcealed

ambidextrous	omnipotent	antifreeze
multiform	anticlimax	omnipresence
multilateral	miniskirt	semiweekly
omnipresent	antibody	semisweet
omnibus	antitrust	semicircle

1   Daniel is familiar with the rules.

2   My dog is a springer spaniel.

3   Please don't put onions on my sandwich.

4   The state of California gets lots of sunshine.

5   Pennsylvania and Virginia were two of the first United States.

6   One trillion is a huge number.

7   Let's get the children's opinion before we make a decision.

8   That is a brilliant solution!

9   The gardenia is blooming in the garden.

10 Kendra likes to ride the white stallion.

1 Isn't that boy the class champion?

2 Philadelphia is a nice city to visit.

3 The stadium was packed with fans.

4 It is sad to think of the treatment of Indians.

5 This shirt is a medium size.

6 The dancers must practice at the studio.

7 Jake's dad told him to turn down the blaring radio.

8 I enjoyed the show about the outer space aliens.

9 Joyce planted geraniums in her garden this year.

10 Cathy has such obedient children.

1   Bert thinks he can win the billiards match.

2   Ms. Lord brilliantly solved the problem.

3   It's conveniently located across the street.

4   The speeches at the reunion will be made following the dinner.

5   All senior citizens must get respect.

6   His companion will analyze the data.

7   The event will take place at the pavilion.

8   Lorna joined the tenth battalion.

9   I am afraid that may cause further alienation.

10 We've proudly displayed the medallion in the trophy case.

1 The event is far dressier than I expected.

2 Mom gave Pete a minibike for his birthday.

3 The semiformal for our school will be on April seventh.

4 Our team has been victorious in its last five games.

5 Stan is envious of his wife's accomplishments.

6 We plan to have semiweekly meetings soon.

7 We need to add antifreeze before the winter arrives.

8 Let's form a semicircle to do this next activity.

9 I would like to visit the Orient someday.

10 Elizabeth went away for the weekend and stayed at a condominium.

1 Ken developed his claustrophobia long ago.

2 Janet's radiance came through as she gave her presentation to the crowd.

3 It is so much fun planning for the big fiesta.

4 We will have to replace the radiator in our old van.

5 I lack calcium in my diet and really should drink more milk.

6 Jake is ambidextrous and can hit the baseball right-handed as well as left-handed.

7 Heather regretted her obvious mistake.

8 Steven has had cardiac difficulties for several years.

9 Sue is the craftiest person in this class.

10 Dad seems like he's in quite a jovial mood.

Robert E. Lee

Few people are called upon to make as momentous a decision as was Robert E. Lee. As a youth, he learned to make difficult choices. He was the male head-of-the-household at the age of twelve. Yet this could not have prepared him for the decision he would need to make later in his life.

As unrest developed in the country, Abraham Lincoln could foresee an unavoidable war looming. Lincoln asked Lee to command the Union forces. Patriotic Lee, siding with the Union, believed that secession was unconstitutional. In addition, he held an antislavery position, freeing his own slaves. Yet he was unwilling to command an army against the South.

Lee was then approached by Confederate leaders. Would he command their army? Lee was a gentle and peace-loving man. He did not use his sword, except for defense. Lee was also a man of strong heritage and devotion. He loved his home state of Virginia. Lee was tormented over the decision. In the end, his affection for his homeland weighed his decision to accept. Though Lee was not victorious, he is considered a great general in our American history.

ie = /ē/

rookie	fierce	relief
goalie	piece	believe
cashier	frontier	field
prairie	masterpiece	outfield
cookie	brownie	shriek

ie = /ē/

tier	pier	brief
cavalier	diesel	piecemeal
headpiece	siege	relieve
belief	reprieve	genie
premier	pierce	zombie

ie = /ē/

ceiling	deceive	neither
weird	receive	caffeine
sheik	either	Keith
conceit	perceive	conceive
seize	protein	deceit

ie/ei = /ē/

receive	relief	thief
niece	neither	relieve
chief	piece	Keith
field	shriek	fierce
frontier	either	brownie

ei = /ā/

their	vein	rein
veil	surveillance	seine
skein	lei	unveiled
chow mein	surveillance	heinous
feint	beige	reindeer

Mixed

their	believe	cavalier
beige	cashier	pierce
priest	diesel	rein
skein	feint	surveillance
tier	deceit	shield

ie = /ē/

1   May I have a piece of that brownie?

2   Jake received a beautiful sweater as a gift.

3   Dad took the tots to visit the reindeer.

4   It will be difficult to find a piece of cloth to match this chair.

5   Neither Tom nor Harry will make a good chief.

6   I can hardly believe the score of last night's play-off game!

7   The field was covered with mud, but the players continued the game.

8   Gram is preparing pies and cookies for Sunday's celebration.

9   Alaska is considered America's last frontier.

10   Our niece will come to visit again next spring.

ie = /ē/

1 I need to stop and get fuel for this diesel engine.

2 This exciting show is a premier attraction.

3 I won't count the calories in the brownies I've eaten.

4 Sandra applied for a job as a cashier in the grocery store.

5 Jim's shriek was so loud that the neighbor called to check on his safety.

6 Yield to the oncoming traffic and then carefully proceed onto the street.

7 The relief from this extreme heat is finally in sight.

8 The goalie attempted to prevent any goals, but he couldn't withstand the attack.

9 The grieving family will return home.

10 I think that the premier film was too unrealistic.

1   Mom preferred the beige coat for Carolyn.

2   Their home is currently on the market for a reasonable price.

3   I drank too much caffeine and now I'm very jumpy.

4   The museum plans to unveil the valued piece of art at the banquet.

5   Keith needs to increase his protein intake.

6   We can order chicken chow mein from the Chinese restaurant.

7   He is a trickster and will deceive us whenever possible.

8   Since Sandy became class queen, she has had a conceited attitude.

9   I believe we should seize this opportunity.

10   That king reigned for three decades.

The Hockey Play-Off

Charlie and Neil stood in line at the fast-food restaurant. They ordered a big box of fried chicken. Then they hurried out the door toward their destination. Charlie had two tickets to the hockey play-off game!

The Star Spangled Banner played as Charlie and Neil found their seats. They were located high in the rafters, almost touching the ceiling! Charlie had tried to find better tickets, but he was actually lucky to seize these imperfect ones.

The game involved a fierce battle between two excellent teams. Gerry, the premier goalie for the home team, had reported slight cold symptoms. Despite this, he started the game. He was able to shield the goal until the second period. Then, two quick scores put the home team behind. The back-up goaltender then relieved Gerry from the net.

Either team could win the contest. It was an exciting match-up, with constant action. The home team fired two goals to tie the score. In the last few moments of the game, the best lines were on the ice. With two minutes left, the center on the away team slid the puck under the goalie's pads. The final score was 3-2. Though the outcome was a disappointment, Charlie and Neil were glad they saw the tension-filled play-off game.

A Big Find

On January 24, 1848, a man by the name of James Marshall was working on a sawmill for his boss, John Sutter. Mr. Sutter was a prosperous soldier of fortune who had developed a vast estate in the frontier land of California. Early in the morning, Marshall was performing a tedious task at the sawmill. Mixed in with gravel, John saw pea-size particles that gave off a dull glitter. He and his boss, Mr. Sutter, could hardly believe it. The pieces of glitter were pure gold!

Marshall and Sutter tried to keep this quiet, but their secret soon spread throughout California. Within weeks the gold fields were covered with fortune seekers hoping to achieve wealth. By 1849, the news had been confirmed in the East. People seized the opportunity to head for the unknown land.

The trip to California was long and difficult. People could take the safest route by boat, but this took months. Others went overland by wagon train. They met danger crossing mountains, prairies, and deserts.

When people arrived in California, they were shocked by what they found. Towns were thrown together to serve the needs of the gold seekers. Thieves were abundant. Supplies were expensive. Few people became rich from their troubles. Many people lost what they once had in search of wealth. John Sutter was among those who did not benefit from the big find. He lost claim to his land and, in the end, died a poor man.

tight	night	light
fight	flight	delight
highway	moonlight	sigh
bright	high	might
headlight	nightmare	lightning

igh

plight	mighty	thigh
fright	alight	fortnight
delightful	enlighten	limelight
foresight	nightingale	frighten
insight	delighted	twilight

eight	sleigh	neighbor
weightless	weight	freight
eighty	neighborhood	weigh
eighteen	freighter	neigh
weighty	neighborly	inveigh

Nonsense Words

bligh	dight	fleighp
cighf	preight	cheigh
inveight	trighn	dreight
spligh	redight	breigh
clight	dreight	bleight

1   Drive on the highway to go to the park.

2   Did the thunder and lightning make you jump?

3   The headlights on that car are bright.

4   When I was six, my dad took me on an airplane flight.

5   Our team just might win the next game.

6   The boys had a fight at recess.

7   The basketball net seems much too high.

8   At the sight of his master, the dog ran in circles.

9   It was such a delightful afternoon.

10   The highway was brightly lit by several street lights.

1 Jenny likes to be in the limelight as much as possible.

2 The meeting with the company president was delightful.

3 Could that sound be a nightingale?

4 Mrs. Philbin had an interesting insight.

5 It will be a fortnight before I can visit.

6 The accident was a frightful sight.

7 I am afraid Henry has a difficult plight.

8 Paula awoke during a terrible nightmare and then could not get back to sleep.

9 That dungaree skirt is much too tight but Kerry insists on getting it!

10 I will try that exercise program to reduce my thighs.

1   The huge freighter will transport the cargo.

2   Noni is over eighty but she still lives alone.

3   Barney must weigh at least fifty pounds.

4   That loud neigh came from the big old barn.

5   The freight train stops at this station at three p.m. every day.

6   In the pool, Kim seemed weightless when I lifted her underwater.

7   The neighbors were so helpful when the barn burned down.

8   Francis is planning a big celebration for Tim's eighteenth birthday.

9   It is a tradition in our family to go for a sleigh ride on New Year's Eve at twilight.

10   Roy sighed as he packed his last bag and left his old neighborhood to relocate.

Nancy's Novel

Nancy was sprawled out on the living room couch. For the first time in her life, she had found a book that interested her so much she could not put it down. It was the first novel she had ever attempted. It was funny and romantic. Nancy was truly enjoying it.

It was a story about Martin Night. He was a teenager in a small Vermont town in 1790. Martin was deeply in love with his neighbor, Sandra Jennings. In the story, Martin and Sandra had an argument in the town center. As a result, Sandra was unavailable for a week. Martin lacked confidence, yet he wanted to see her so much, he had to plot something.

Nancy turned the pages with anticipation. It was now eight o'clock at night and she had plans to go out with a friend at eight-thirty. She did not want to wait until the next day to find out what would happen.

Nancy felt she could see the small Vermont town in her mind. She understood the hardships of farm life because the description in the book gave such detail. She continued reading. (continued)

Nancy's Novel (continued)

Martin had a plan. It was a bright December evening. He went into his barn and attached the horses to the sleigh. The moon was full and high in the sky. He sat in the sleigh for awhile as he got up his nerve to go to his neighbor's house and request that Sandra go come with him for a ride in the moonlight.

As Martin drove the two miles along the dirt road, he went over and over how he was going to ask Mr. Jennings if Sandra could go for the ride. He prayed that she would go!

Just then, the doorbell at Nancy's house rang loudly. It made her jump! Her friend was there to go out. She wanted to hurry and finish the chapter in the book, but her friend did not want to hang around.

Nancy gave a sigh. She would have to wait to find out whether or not Sandra would accept Martin's invitation. Nancy was delighted to enjoy a book so much!

Post Test Step 11

A

pennies	piano	hurried
stadium	enjoyable	symptom
gymnastic	copied	supply
studying	onion	moonlight
achieve	neighbor	turkeys

B

nastier	cardiogram	beige
symphonist	portrayed	freighter
supplying	glorious	semiconductor
enzyme	brilliant	denied
recipient	deceit	claustrophobia

Post Test Step 11

Nonsense Words

shymp	semidrome	prystal
murvoyed	strillion	shomious
conboyable	spyle	ploggiest
benion	clobier	libneying
delpiant	preshyme	bryllor

1 Mark the **y** in closed syllables (A + B) and **y-e** syllables (B).

2 Highlight any **i** that makes the consonant sound of **y**.

3 Put an **e** over each **i** that is pronounced /ē/ in words <u>without</u> suffixes.

4 Circle all suffixes.

5 Put a box around the **ie/ei** and **eigh** vowel combinations and identify the sound.

6 Fill in the chart below with any word that has suffix additions.

word	base	suffix	drop y, change to i	keep y, add suffix
replied	reply	-ed		
donkeys	donkey	-s		